# The Grump

BY LUCY FLOYD

ILLUSTRATIONS BY STEVE SANFORD

# Harcourt Brace & Company

Orlando  Atlanta  Austin  Boston  San Francisco  Chicago  Dallas  New York  Toronto  London

Mom told me, "Don't jump
in the pond."

Jed told me, "Don't dump
sand on my hand."

Dad told me, "Don't
tramp sand in here."

Pat told me, "Don't slump.
Sit up."

Jill told me, "Don't bump
the lamp."

Don't jump, dump, tramp,
slump, bump.
Don't, don't, don't!
That always makes me
a grump.

7

Then they all told me,
"Don't be a grump!"

What's a child to do?

Well, I'll find Gramp.

Gramp knows I jump,
dump, tramp, slump, and
bump. Gramp knows I'm a
grump, too.
But Gramp doesn't mind.

Gramp always thinks
I'm a champ.